Everest Adventures

Written by Claire Owen

Nepal

My name is Barati. I live in a small village in the mountains of Nepal. Have you ever been on the very top of a mountain peak? If so, how high was that mountain? Would you like to climb the tallest peak in the world? Why or why not?

Contents

Wherever you see me, you'll find activities to try and questions to answer.

Mighty Mountains

The world's highest peaks are in the mountain range known as the Himalayas, or "place of snow." With 14 peaks that are more than 8,000 meters above sea level, the Himalaya mountain range is about 2,400 kilometers long and 400 kilometers wide. It stretches from Pakistan and northern India through Nepal and Bhutan to Tibet, in southern China. Eight of the world's ten tallest mountains are in Nepal.

A view of the Himalayas from 350 kilometers above Earth

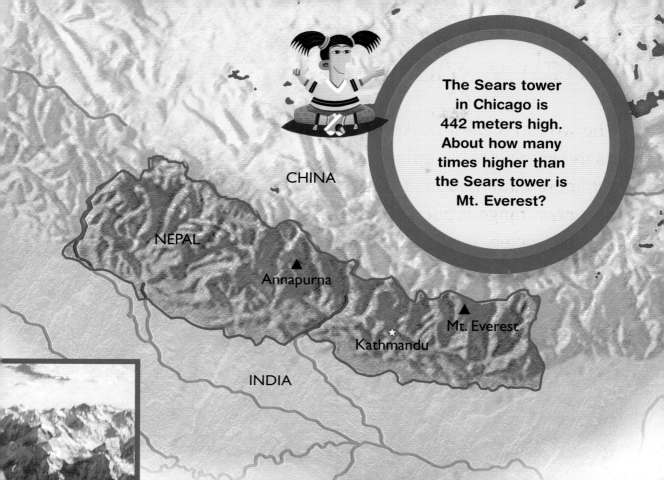

CHINA

NEPAL

Annapurna ▲

Mt. Everest ▲

★ Kathmandu

INDIA

The Sears tower in Chicago is 442 meters high. About how many times higher than the Sears tower is Mt. Everest?

World's Top Ten Mountains

Mountain	Height (Meters)
Mt. Everest	8,850
K2	8,611
Kanchenjunga	8,586
Lhotse	8,516
Makalu	8,463
Cho Oyu	8,201
Dhaulagiri	8,167
Manaslu	8,163
Nanga Parbat	8,125
Annapurna	8,091

What's in a Name?

Two centuries ago, the Andes in South America were thought to be the tallest mountains in the world. In the early 1800s, British surveyors began making an accurate map of India. When the surveyors reached the Himalayas, they used Roman numerals to name the peaks. In 1852, they decided that Peak XV was the highest mountain on Earth. In 1865, Peak XV was renamed Mt. Everest, after one of the leaders of the survey.

The Great Trigonometric Survey of India was begun in 1802 and completed in 1866. The surveyors measured the country from south to north, a distance of more than 2,400 kilometers.

trigonometric   related to the branch of mathematics that deals with relations between the sides and angles of triangles

Surveyors use an instrument called a *theodolite* to measure the angle to the top of a mountain. It is set over a fixed point and has a telescope that pivots up, down, and across.

The theodolite used in India weighed about 500 kilograms. It took 12 men to carry it.

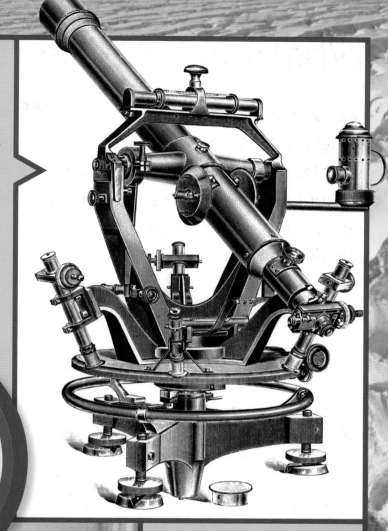

How many years ago was Peak XV declared the highest mountain? How many years ago was it renamed Mt. Everest?

Sir George Everest pronounced his name *Eev-rest* rather than *Ever-est*. It is believed that he retired without ever having seen the mountain that was named after him.

Measuring a Mountain

In 1856, British surveyors calculated that the height of Mt. Everest was 8,840 meters. In 1955, the official height was adjusted to 8,848 meters. On May 5, 1999, climbers carrying GPS satellite equipment measured the height at 8,850 meters. Although these changes were mainly due to more accurate ways of measuring, Mt. Everest is actually growing taller by about one centimeter each year. This is due to movement in Earth's crust.

Mt. Everest

GPS   Global Positioning System

When mountains are measured from the center of Earth rather than from sea level, Everest is not the tallest peak. The summit of Chimborazo in Ecuador is 6,384,459 meters from the center of Earth, compared with Everest at 6,382,279 meters.

Mauna Kea, an active volcano in Hawaii, has a height of 4,170 meters above sea level. However, the base of the mountain is 5,998 meters below sea level, on the ocean floor. This makes Mauna Kea the tallest mountain, from base to summit.

What is the difference in height of Chimborazo and Everest, measured from the center of Earth? How high is Mauna Kea, from base to summit?

On Top of the World

Many mountaineers wanted to be the first to climb
Mt. Everest. However, Nepal's borders were closed to
outsiders from 1846 to 1950. Beginning in 1921, seven
British expeditions tried to climb Everest from the north,
via Tibet. All of these attempts failed, and twelve men lost
their lives. After two more unsuccessful expeditions from the
Nepal side in the early 1950s, Edmund Hillary from
New Zealand and Tenzing Norgay from Nepal reached
the summit of Everest on May 29, 1953.

Edmund Hillary and Tenzing Norgay

expedition   a journey made for a special purpose

The 1953 Route

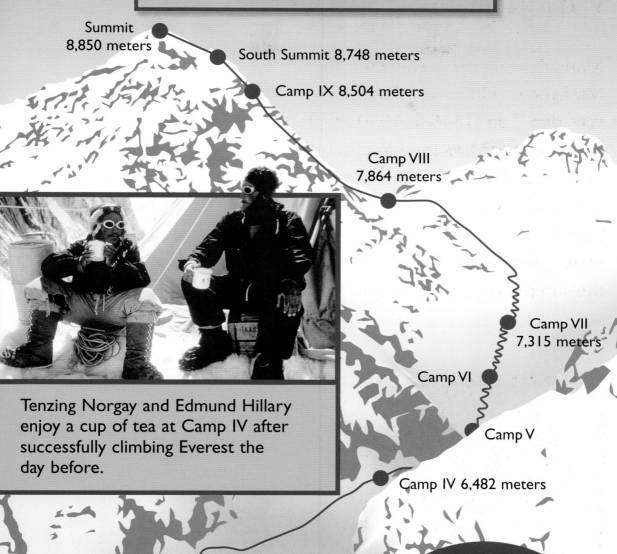

Summit
8,850 meters

South Summit 8,748 meters

Camp IX 8,504 meters

Camp VIII
7,864 meters

Camp VII
7,315 meters

Camp VI

Camp V

Camp IV 6,482 meters

Camp III

Camp II

Tenzing Norgay and Edmund Hillary enjoy a cup of tea at Camp IV after successfully climbing Everest the day before.

Pick one of the heights above. How many meters below the summit is it? Now pick two heights. What is the difference between them?

Base Camp 5,456 meters

Because It's There

After they conquered Everest in 1953, Hillary and Tenzing thought that no one would ever make another attempt to climb the mountain—but they were wrong! In the 50 years that followed, about 10,000 people tried to reach the summit. About 1,660 successful ascents were made by more than 1,200 people from 63 countries.

In the year 2004 alone, 330 people reached the summit. This was 45 more than in the 1950s, 1960s, 1970s, and 1980s combined!

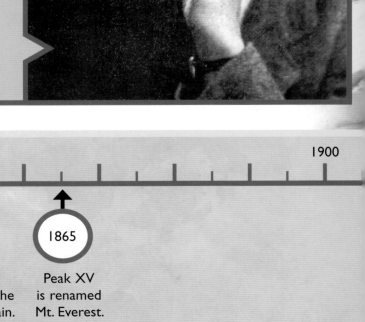

When asked why he wanted to climb Everest, mountaineer George Mallory replied, "Because it's there." Mallory died on Everest in 1924. His body was not found until 1999.

1850   1900

1852
Peak XV is
recognized as the
highest mountain.

1865
Peak XV
is renamed
Mt. Everest.

On Mt. Everest each year, new records are set or old records broken. In 2001, for example, 89 climbers reached the summit on the same day! In 2003, a 70-year-old man became the oldest person to climb Everest.

Pick two dates on the chart. Figure out the number of years, months, and days between those dates.

Summit "Firsts"

• American	May 1, 1963
• To reach the summit twice	May 20, 1965
• Woman	May 16, 1975
• In winter	Feb. 17, 1980
• Solo	Aug. 20, 1980
• Descent on a paraglider	Sep. 26, 1988
• Son of a summiter	May 10, 1990
• Married couple (together)	Oct. 7, 1990
• Father and son (together)	Oct. 7, 1990
• Brothers (together)	Sep. 25, 1992
• Sleep on the summit	May 6, 1999
• Descent on skis	Oct. 7, 2000
• Descent on a snowboard	May 24, 2001
• Blind person	May 25, 2001
• One-armed climber	May 23, 2003

1950

1921

The first attempt to climb Everest is made.

May 29, 1953

Hillary and Tenzing reach the summit.

May 8, 1978

The first ascent without bottled oxygen is made.

13

Into Thin Air

Climbing Mt. Everest presents many challenges. Even in summer, wind speeds on the mountain can reach 150 kilometers per hour, and the temperature can drop to –40°C. An ever-present danger for mountaineers is the shortage of oxygen. At the summit of Everest, the air pressure is about one-third of the pressure at sea level. This means that there is only one-third as much oxygen to breathe.

Most people who climb Everest use bottled oxygen. However, since 1978, more than 100 climbers have reached the summit without using bottled oxygen.

People cannot survive for very long in air pressures below 50 kiloPascals (kPa). At the summit of Mt. Everest, the air pressure is not much more than 30 kiloPascals. Lack of oxygen causes shortness of breath, headaches, and nosebleeds. Climbers can become disoriented and suffer from hallucinations.

Use the line graph to determine the air pressure at sea level (0 meters). About how much is it at 5,000 meters? At what altitude is the air pressure about 60 kiloPascals?

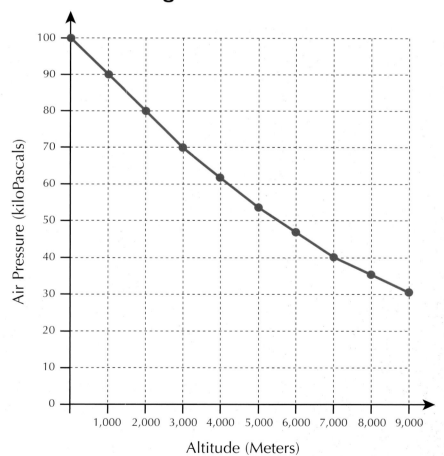

How Air Pressure Changes with Height Above Sea Level

Air Pressure (kiloPascals)

Altitude (Meters)

Counting the Cost

In the 1950s, only the world's most experienced mountaineers attempted to climb Mt. Everest. More recently, however, some people with relatively little climbing experience have reached the summit. These people pay up to $65,000 to join an expedition with experienced guides who help them make it to the top. Additional costs—for items such as high-altitude clothing, climbing equipment, airfare, and a satellite phone—can easily amount to another $15,000.

More than 150 Himalayan peaks are open to climbers. The cost of a mountaineering permit depends on the height of the mountain. A special fee is charged to climb Mt. Everest.

Mountaineering Permits

Height (Meters)	Cost for up to 7 people	Each extra person
5,500–6,500	$1,500	$200
6,501–7,000	$2,000	$300
7,001–7,500	$3,000	$400
7,501–8,000	$4,000	$500
Over 8,000	$10,000	$1,500
Everest (normal route)	$70,000	$10,000

permit   an official document giving permission to do something

Figure It Out

Answer the first two questions below for each of these peaks.
a. Khiuri Khala (5,806 meters)
b. Api (7,132 meters)
c. Kanchenjunga (8,586 meters)

1. Find the cost of a mountaineering permit for a group of 12 people.

2. If the 12 people in the group split the cost of the permit equally, how much would each person pay? (Round your answer to the nearest cent.)

3. Now find the cost of a permit for 12 people to climb Mt. Everest.

4. Pick one of the three peaks above (a, b, or c). How much more does the permit for Everest cost than the permit for that peak?

Taking It Easier

Not everyone wants to climb Mt. Everest! Many visitors to Nepal enjoy trekking in the mountains below the base camp, or in other scenic areas of the country. Because of the high altitude, trekkers usually walk for only three or four hours each day, carrying a light pack. Along the way, they can enjoy the views, visit the Buddhist monasteries, and stay at the teahouses.

scenic   having beautiful scenery

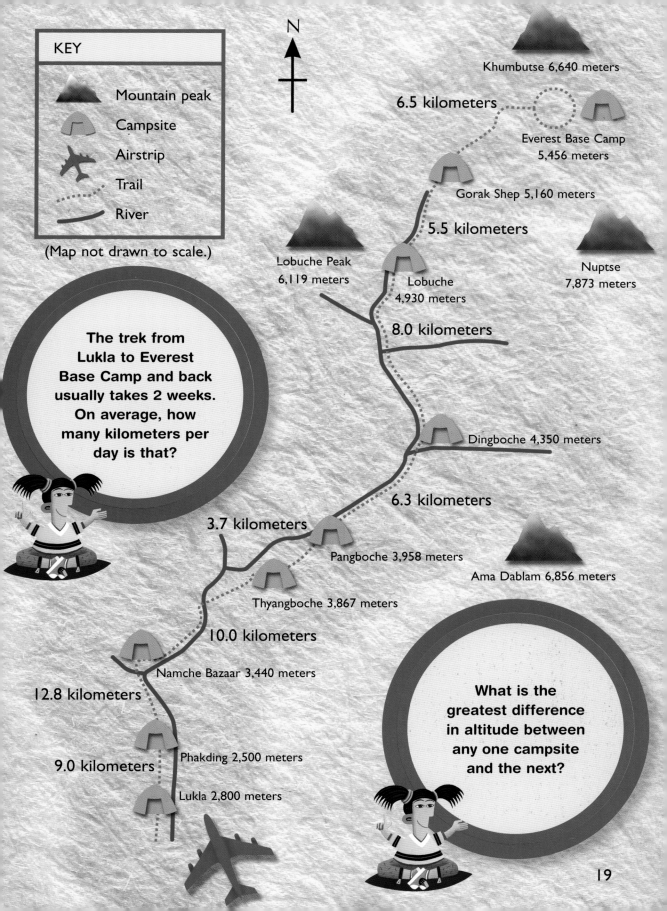

KEY

- 🏔 Mountain peak
- ⛺ Campsite
- ✈ Airstrip
- ⋯ Trail
- ～ River

(Map not drawn to scale.)

N

Khumbutse 6,640 meters

6.5 kilometers

Everest Base Camp 5,456 meters

Gorak Shep 5,160 meters

5.5 kilometers

Lobuche Peak 6,119 meters

Lobuche 4,930 meters

Nuptse 7,873 meters

8.0 kilometers

The trek from Lukla to Everest Base Camp and back usually takes 2 weeks. On average, how many kilometers per day is that?

Dingboche 4,350 meters

6.3 kilometers

3.7 kilometers

Pangboche 3,958 meters

Ama Dablam 6,856 meters

Thyangboche 3,867 meters

10.0 kilometers

Namche Bazaar 3,440 meters

12.8 kilometers

What is the greatest difference in altitude between any one campsite and the next?

Phakding 2,500 meters

9.0 kilometers

Lukla 2,800 meters

Raising Revenue

Nepal is among the poorest nations in the world, and revenue from trekking and mountain climbing plays an important part in the country's economy. In 1995, for example, permits for mountaineering, trekking, and entry to national parks raised more than $3.3 million. Today, visitors to Nepal spend more than $100 million each year and provide employment for thousands of people.

Typically, 12 climbers will need about 3 metric tons of food and gear. They will employ about 30 porters, 12 climbing Sherpas, 10 cooks, 12 yak herders, and 75 yaks!

Sherpa a member of a Himalayan people living in Nepal and Tibet

Revenue from Permits (1995)

Type of Permit	Number Sold	Revenue
Mountaineering	624	$571,500
Trekking Peak*	3,046	$150,000
Trekking	84,787	$805,735
Park Entry	136,142	$1,819,092
Total	224,599	$3,346,327

* Trekking Peak permits are climbing permits for some
of Nepal's less challenging peaks.

Which pie chart
matches the data in
the Revenue column
above? ... the Number Sold
column? Use a calculator
to find the average
cost of each kind
of permit.

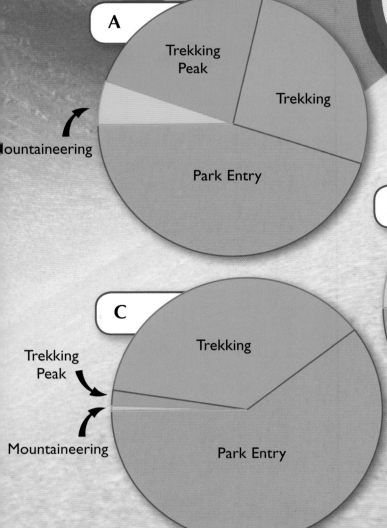

A

Trekking
Peak

Trekking

Mountaineering

Park Entry

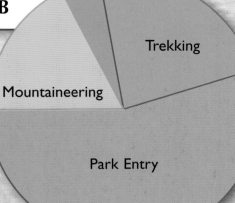

Trekking Peak

B

Trekking

Mountaineering

Park Entry

C

Trekking
Peak

Trekking

Mountaineering

Park Entry

Protecting Everest

The number of expeditions to Everest each year is increasing, and some people are concerned that this is damaging the environment. Until a recent clean-up, the mountain was littered with used oxygen cylinders and other trash. Although the high cost of a climbing permit helps to limit the number of expeditions, some people feel that there should be stricter controls on the number of climbers each season. They want to make sure that climbing the world's highest peak will always be a very special experience.

Number of Climbers Reaching the Summit of Everest Each Year							
1953	2	1966	0	1979	18	1992	90
1954	0	1967	0	1980	10	1993	129
1955	0	1968	0	1981	5	1994	51
1956	4	1969	0	1982	18	1995	83
1957	0	1970	4	1983	23	1996	98
1958	0	1971	0	1984	17	1997	85
1959	0	1972	0	1985	30	1998	120
1960	3	1973	10	1986	4	1999	117
1961	0	1974	0	1987	2	2000	146
1962	0	1975	15	1988	50	2001	182
1963	6	1976	4	1989	24	2002	159
1964	0	1977	2	1990	72	2003	264
1965	9	1978	25	1991	38	2004	330

Make a Bar Graph

You will need a copy of the Blackline Master and colored markers.

1. In the first column, color a bar to represent the 2 climbers who climbed Everest in 1953.

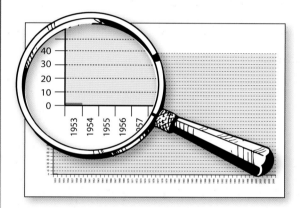

2. Leave the columns for 1954 and 1955 blank. Then color a bar to show the 4 climbers in 1956.

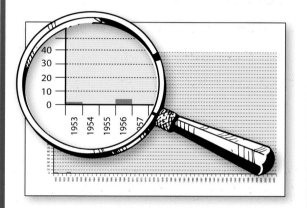

3. Continue in a similar way for each of the other years in the chart on page 22.

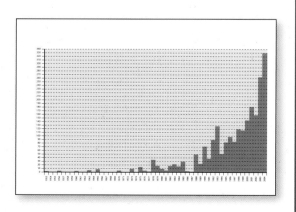

4. Now write a suitable title for your graph and label each axis.

Title

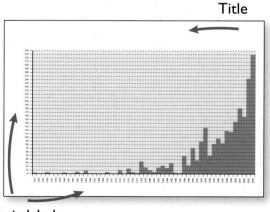

Axis labels

Sample Answers

Find out the altitude where you live. Compare that altitude to the height of Mt. Everest and other peaks, such as the tallest peak in your state, country, or continent.

Page 5   about 20 times as high

Page 9   2,180 meters   10,168 meters

Page 15   about 100 kiloPascals;

about 53 kiloPascals;

about 4,200 meters

Page 17
1. a. $2,500   b. $5,000
    c. $17,500
2. a. $208.33   b. $416.67
    c. $1,458.33
3. $120,000
4. a. $117,500 b. $115,000
    c. $102,500

Page 19   about 9 km per day

(123.6 km ÷ 14 days)

940 meters (Phakding, Namche Bazaar)

Page 21   Revenue: B; Number Sold: C

$915.87, $49.24, $9.50, $13.36

Index